Soul Beautiful

*Create in me a clean heart, O God, and renew
a right Spirit within me. Psalms 51:10*

"Beauty Tips For Your Soul"

by

Diane W. Pheal

ISBN: 1-4107-5011-6 (e-book)
ISBN: 1-4107-5010-8 (Paperback)
ISBN: 1-4107-5009-4 (Dust Jacket)

This book is printed on acid free paper.

1stBooks - rev. 6/5/03

A book dedicated to guiding you through soul beautification by using familiar outward beautification processes.

Dedication

To my Father in heaven, the creator and giver of all things, I thank you! I thank god for the gifts He so lovingly bestowed upon me, for choosing me, for using me. God has inspired me to do this work so that others can be blessed, encouraged, and enlightened. I acknowledge to the world that I am truly nothing without Him and in Him I live, move and have my being.

To my parents, Mom (deceased), Daddy, thank you for all the encouragement, training and other benefits you provided. Thank you for being loving and concerned parents who first and above all taught us to love God. To my sisters, brothers, my sons and all who have been a source of encouragement, I thank you. I dare not forget my best friends, you know who you are, I love you all.

Finally, to all my sisters in Christ, I thank God for you and pray this will be a blessing to you.

In Christ,

Diane

Table of Contents

How to Use This Guide

This guide is to be used with the Holy Bible. It's intent is to show you how to take the outward beautification process and put it to work for you during your inward beautification process. Please note that this is a life long process and cannot be achieved overnight, although some changes may possibly occur overnight after sincere prayer has been offered up. But the actual beautification process will become a daily ritual.

I suggest that you read this book in its entirety, go back to the first process and prayerfully put it to work. You already have the Holy Spirit to aid you, now you just need to put him to work for you.

This will not be an easy process but you must be faithful to it and "commit to be committed to it."

Preface

It is the calling and gifts of God on a person's life that brings them into the ministry of the Lord. Your sex has nothing to do with it. As you dedicate yourself to the Lord and seek His face, you will be prepared to fulfill His will for your life. The beauty of Christ is seen in the Fruit of the Spirit. A life touched by Christ will show a Godly character. True spiritual maturity is measured by the Fruit of the Spirit and not the gifts of the Holy Spirit. Gifts are what God gives us, whereas the fruit of the Holy Spirit is what we give to God by yielding to the Holy Spirit and allowing Him to touch our personality and character. 1 Peter 3:3—4 "Do no let your adornment be *merely* outward—arranging the hair, wearing gold, or putting on *fine* apparel; rather *let it be* the hidden person of the heart, with the incorruptible *beauty* of a gentle and quiet spirit, which is very precious in the sight of God. (NKJV) Under the New Testament, the Holy Spirit still prepares us to be beautiful in the sight of God. ***This is inner beauty!*** Are you allowing God to give you a beauty treatment? If you **_truly_** want to be beautiful on the inside, read on. The only beauty tool you will need is your **Bible**.

There is so much that God wants for us. He wants to be the center of our lives. But before He can use us, we must go through a beautification process...much has to be done on the inside.

We must dedicate more time to cleansing the inside with the only pure cleansing ingredient ever—God's Word! Not only will we be cleansed on the inside, we will notice that we are losing weight. All those things that burden us down will gradually fall by the wayside. The weight of our past, the guilt, unforgiveness, envy, worry, lack of faith, weakness, and so many other things that puts a burden on our soul. Just like the fatty foods that we eat that cause us to gain weight (and we blame it on those foods), Satan is just as responsible for the negative thoughts that he sends to us. Because we listen, we develop a lack of faith and tend to carry our own burdens rather that "casting them upon the Lord." But as we go through the renewal process, we will find ourselves shedding those weights and encasing ourselves in the Word of God which provides the protection we need from the enemy.

The world sees only the outside and judges us by our outward beauty, but God looks into the heart, the seat of our emotions, and begins his reformation process from within and works outwardly. There is only so much we can do with the outward beauty, but the inner beauty can continuously be enhanced. As this inward transformation takes place, it gradually shows in our daily lives, outshining the outward beauty.

I pray this book will give you the courage to open your hearts to receive what God has to offer you. As you begin to surrender to the *relaxing massage* of His Holy Word, *exercise* it daily and you will feel a change happening within. A warmth and a new spirit will evolve.

Be blessed and always be a "Woman Walking in Wisdom!

Diane Pheal

Soul

"My soul thirsteth for God, for the living God: Psalms 42:2a

What is the Soul? We could say that it is the "breath of life" for the soul gives life to the physical body. The body itself still needs to breath to maintain life. The soul is breath in itself. It continues to live even though the body dies. The soul enables us to *"walk in the Spirit."*

As Christians we do experience a struggle within. "For the flesh lusteth against the Spirit, and the Spirit against the flesh." People can and will inflict pain upon us. They can cause suffering and even death. But the good news is that no person can harm our souls. The soul does get weary and needs to be restored. This affirmation comes to us in Psalms 23: when the psalmist says, "he restoreth my soul." In his healing voice, Jesus bids us saying "Come unto me all ye that labor and are heavy laden, and I will give you rest (Matthew 11:28). Our souls are under the protection of God himself. Nothing can penetrate the protective shield that surrounds us. As we journey through this life, we must put our trust in God and praise him for his word and his work in our lives. God is our refuge and He covers us with his feathers. Nothing can harm us for he has given his angels charge over us. Our souls are filled with his love and promises.

"The Lord is my light and my salvation, whom shall I fear? the Lord is the strength of my life; of whom shall I be afraid?" (Psalms 27:1) Confidence in God is seen in where we look for help in our time of need. "I will lift up mine

eyes unto the hills, from whence cometh my help. My help
cometh from the Lord, who made heaven and earth."
(Psalm 121: 1—2) The help we need, God will send, in His
own way and His own time. If He doesn't send it, no one
can help, but also, if He sends it, no one can hinder it. We
must encourage our confidence in God. All those things we
fear, God tells us not to be afraid. God, who created all
things, has given us the ability to speak resolution to our
troubles and fears.   By giving ourselves over for his
protection and pledging our daily "devotion" (being
devoted) to him, we will be kept safe. The Lord, our good
Shepherd preserves us from the evil of sin and trouble. Not
to say we won't have these but he protects us from the
devastating effects of these. Everything that is aimed at us
must go through God first.   God takes the Spiritual life
under his protection—he protects the soul. All souls are his
and therefore He takes special care to preserve them from
being defiled by sin and *disturbed by affliction*. When our
souls are in a tempest storm, we should run to the Lord so
that He can calm the storm. Spiritual bondage can cause us
to have great storms of doubt and fear in our souls. When
we understand who God truly is, we will realize that He
controls both the storms of nature and the storms of a
troubled soul. Our faith should insure us that God **can** and
will meet our needs.

   Don't waste your time on the vain things of this world.
Things that you get caught up in are not the proper food for
your soul because there is no nourishment. If you listen to
Christ you will eat that which is good, wholesome and
pleasant, good in itself and good for you. The scripture
says, "Hear and your soul shall live." (Isaiah 55:3b) The
Words of God are ***Spirit*** and ***Life***!

How does the soul receive its nourishment? By seeking the Lord through prayer, by daily reading His word, meditating on the word and listening for His voice. When God asks "What would you have me to do for you today? ask what you will.

> Ask to be reconciled to him if it is needed
> Ask to be better acquainted with him
> Ask for your portion of joy
> Ask for your healing
> Ask for forgiveness and express your sorrow
> Ask him to create in you a clean heart
> Ask for guidance of the Holy Spirit
> Ask Him to rule your life
> Ask Him to bless you with his anointing

Give Him everything and then be thankful to him for being in His favor, and for his mercy.

God is waiting to hear from you. His word is constantly calling us and His Spirit is striving with us. He is pleading to us to accept Him and the wonderful blessings He has in store for us.

Note: If you feel the need to fast at anytime during your inner beauty renewal process, please choose the fast that God has chosen for us which consists of reforming our whole lives and undoing what we have done by mistake or wrongly. ***But be careful when fasting—true repentance comes from "within", it is not an outward show.*** Know that the purpose for fasting is usually in connection with penitence, mourning and supplication—self-denial that

3

opens you to God. Fastening gives believers an opportunity to express themselves in an undivided and intensive devotion to the Lord and the concerns of the Spiritual Life.

Soul

What is the Soul?

What does Psalms 27:1 speak to you?

How does the soul receive nourishment?

What is the purpose of fastening?

Diane W. Pheal

Looking Our Best

Each of us wants to be beautiful. Our appearance is important and we spend hundreds of thousands of dollars yearly on cleansing and beauty products for the face and body. Department stores, beauty supply stores and drug stores carry an array of items geared to meet the demands of purchased advertised products. We spend uncounted minutes on our hair, face and body to make ourselves presentable and attractive. What we have failed to remind ourselves of is that "beauty begins on the inside of a person". But how do we begin to develop our inner beauty. Patience, kindness and joy begins the beauty process that help us become truly beautiful on the inside.

Some Christian women try to gain respect by looking beautiful rather than becoming Christ like in character. It is not unscriptural for a woman to want to be attractive but we need to focus as much energy on our inner beauty as we do on our outward beauty. A gentle and loving character gives a radiance to the face that cannot be duplicated by the best cosmetics. A carefully groomed exterior is artificial and cold if inner beauty is not present.

God wants us to be good workers for him. He is concerned about the quality and beauty of what we do for Him. Therefore, good workers take pride in the quality of work they do. We cannot be good workers for God if our focus is only on our outward appearance.

In order for us to be beautiful on the inside, we must follow a regimen that will purge impurities and replace any and all things that are contrary to God's will for our lives.

In order to do this we must give ourselves completely to him, **mentally, physically and spiritually.**

Yes, we all want to look our best, but looking our best should be for God and not for man.

Let's begin our process by removing our makeup.

Process #1
Eye and Make-up Remover
(The Word of God)

"And he humbled thee, and suffered thee to hunger, and fed thee with manna, which thou knewest not, neither did thy fathers know; that he might make thee know that man doth not live by bread only, but by every word that proceedeth out of the mouth of the Lord doth a man live."
(Deuteronomy 8:3)

Jesus quoted this verse when Satan tempted him to turn stones into bread (Matthew 4:4). Too many people think that life is based on satisfying their appetites or having the abundance of things. They think that if they can earn enough money to acquire things, they are "living the good life." The **"good life"** does not consist of the abundance of "things", because these things do not satisfy the soul. **"Real life"** or the **"good life"** comes from total commitment to God. It requires discipline, sacrifice and hard work, which is why most people never find it. This is when we need to use the **"Eye and Make-up Remover"**. Most people use creams or oils to remove make-up at the end of the day and once they have cleansed their face, the true person stands before them. All the flaws reappear because they are no longer covered. When we put on our make-up people only see the outward beauty. The drawback in this is that most of us refuse to be seen "without" our make-up because people will see in truth, what we really look like. When we are truly honest with ourselves, we will see who we really are. God's Word works the same way as it does it's beautification process within. When we use the *"cream of his word"* and the *"oil of his promises"* we began to remove what we falsely portray and allow the inner realness that God is transforming us into to exhale.

When we use God's Word to cream off all the inner make-up we have spent years applying, we are gradually polishing our personalities and characters. More than that, we become more sensitive to God's every move and word because of the purification we are going through and the effect it has on our ears and eyes. The cleansing process is painful, but necessary in order for us to be totally submitted to God's service. We must be cleansed inwardly so that we can truly represent God who is *pure* and *holy*. Our *remover* is Jesus Christ and His word. His death on the cross removed all sins past and present. When we accepted Him as our Savior and Lord, the transformation process began. However, our selfish desires and deeds soon became the make-up that covered us on the inside. So thick that nothing but the grace of God could penetrate. God's remover works long and deep to reveal a stronger character, peace of mind and deep (down in the soul) satisfaction.

The "oil of God's promises" ensures us that "if God said it, that settles it." Matthew 25:35 assures us of this: "Heaven and earth shall pass away, but my words shall not pass away." God's Word is not for our *information* but rather our *transformation*. Colossians 1:6 tells us "Which is come unto you, as it is in all the world: and bringeth forth fruit, as it doth also in you, since the day ye heard of it, and knew the grace of God in truth." When hard hearts are oiled with the word, a softening takes place. We begin a new relationship with God, and rather than just turning over a new leaf, we become a new person. We are now living in reality and truth. We have made a change in our direction, purpose, attitudes and behavior.

If we are sincere about change, if we want to be real and "live the good life" we must be receptive to God's Word and the change it can generate. A change that will be felt on the inside and seen on the outside. Christians still have the capacity to sin. The good news is that we are no longer enslaved by our old sinful nature. Our eyes have been opened and we can see sin for what it is—the barrier between us and God. God's word is truth and power and helps us to see ourselves for who we really are. The two-edged sword mentioned in Hebrews 4:12 reveals two things to us: *who we really are and who we are not!* It penetrates the core of our moral and spiritual lives, discerning what is really within us, which is both good and evil. God's Word will act like the cleansing agents in the make-up remover. As we listen to His words, we will begin to practice His words and let them shape our lives daily.

Now let's wash our face really good!

Process #1
Eye and Make-up Remover
(The Word of God)

Where does "real life" or the "good life really come from? What is required of you to obtain it?

What is the purpose of God's word?

What does Hebrews 5:12 reveal to you?

Process # 2
Washing
(Attitude)

"All the days of the afflicted are evil: but he that is of a merry heart hath a continual feast. Proverbs 15:15*

After we have removed our make-up (the word of God is truth and shows us who we are), we still need to wash our faces. Normally, we use a washcloth, soap and warm water. This helps to remove leftover make-up, the product used to remove the make-up and allows the pores to breath again. But washing alone will not complete the cleansing process. More steps are needed to begin the restoration process which is needed during our inner beauty treatment.

Our attitudes color our whole personality. We cannot always choose what happens to us, but we can choose our attitude towards each situation. Philippians 4:4-7 gives us the secret: "Rejoice in the Lord always. I will say it again. Rejoice! Let your gentleness be evident to all. The Lord is near. Do not be anxious for anything, but in everything, by prayer and petition, with thanksgiving, present your requests to God. And the peace of God, which transcends all understanding, will guard your hearts and your minds in Christ Jesus." (NIV) Our inner attitudes do not have to be a reflection of our outward circumstances. We are urged to be joyful in all things. God is the source of our joy. There are many who use the words "happy or happiness". Being happy is a temporal feeling. The result of something or someone making us happy for the moment. But joy, real joy, comes from God. Joy within allows you to realize that whatever state you are in, you know that God is the deliverer. Situations nor circumstances can rob you of your joy. Joy within becomes the "attitude dispenser." It dispenses joy when discouragement comes, joy when you are disappointed, joy when there is sorrow, when you are broke, friendless, lonely and joy for any other emotion that you experience in your Christian life. This joy that we have on the inside confuses the world because they don't understand the smile on your faces when all else seems to be going wrong.

Your attitude towards life's situations is vital in your Christian growth because it controls your "reaction." How we react shows *who* is in control, you or the Father. If God is in control you will react in a manner that is truly Christ like, seen or unseen by the world. Your reaction, under Christ's control, to situations will act like a magnet, drawing others to him.

When you turn your attitude and reactions over to God, he will give you peace that transcends all understanding.

Reading God's Word is not all that we need to do to be beautiful. Your attitude towards life proves to the world that you have a power within that helps you when you need it. Many times our attitude surprises even us. There are actions that we must take to walk the road of holiness. The first is to accept and believe that Jesus' blood was the atonement for our sins.

How does blood make an atonement for our sins? Jesus shed his blood for the atonement of our sins. His life, in place of our sins. Jesus' death reconciled us to God, making amends for our sins—it was the cleansing process we desperately needed.

Process #2
Washing
(Attitude)

How we react to situations reflect our character. What does Philippians 4:4-7 have to say about how we are to handle circumstances/situations?

What is the real difference in "happiness" and "joy?"

What "proof" are you showing to the world when your attitude towards circumstances are not what the world expects?

Diane W. Pheal

Process #3
Exfoliate
(Renewing the Mind)

"I beseech you therefore, brethren, by the mercies of God, to present your bodies a living sacrifice, holy and acceptable to God, which is your reasonable service. (Romans 12:1)

When you begin your outward facial cleansing process, you usually begin with an exfoliater. When you exfoliate, you **cast off** the dead skin. This process makes the skin livelier; it looks brighter and feels refreshed. It actually leaves the skin feeling *renewed.*

This is the same process we need to take with our minds. We need to have our minds feeling livelier, brighter and refreshed. The best way to renew or refresh the mind is in your secret place of prayer. When we cast off those temporal things that distract or hinder us, we are able to come into the presence of God and put our minds on the things that are of God. The transforming power of God begins to work first in our minds, for the mind is where sin is first conceived and where doubts first begin.

Satan begins his attacks first in our thoughts, the window through which he enters. But God's Word gives us the strength to slam the window closed in Satan's face. Satan attempts to put discouraging thoughts, doubts, and a feeling of low self-esteem in our minds if we are unable to resist him. We must cast off these disabling thoughts. Our minds must stay focused on the Word of God. As we memorize scriptures we can use the Sword of the Spirit when the enemy attacks. The Sword (Spirit, God's Word) is the only weapon of offense mentioned in Ephesians 6. There are times when we recognize that we are being tempted of Satan and must take the offense against him. To do this, we must bring our thoughts into captivity and trust in God's Word! We must develop the habit of thinking god-ward and gradually, 2 Corinthians 10:5 will be fulfilled: "Casting down imaginations, and every high thing that exalth itself against the knowledge of God, and bringing into captivity every thought into the obedience of Christ." Remember, thoughts and words are seeds. Bad seed can bear fruit in our lives as well as good seed.

You cannot do the exfoliating process alone…you must do this with and by the Word of God. Hebrew 4:12, "For the Word of God is quick (living) and powerful, and sharper than any two-edged sword, piercing to the dividing asunder of soul and spirit, and of the joints and marrow, and is a discerner of the thoughts and intents of the heart." The Word of God is not just a collection of words from God, it is *living, life changing and dynamic* as it works in us. It *penetrates* the *core* of our *moral* and *spiritual lives*. It discerns what is within us, both good and evil. We must not only listen to the Word, but let it mold and shape our lives.

As you begin your study of God's Word, it is suggested that you begin your study in prayer and ask God to give you understanding. "Open thou mine eyes, that I may behold wondrous things out of thy law." (Psalms 119:18) Studying God's Word will help you to "cast off" by restricting you from doing those things that might cripple you and keep you from being your best for him. Your flesh is the "**I**" that tries to satisfy the "**me**" with anything but God's mercy. The identifying mark of the flesh is it's "unsubmissiveness." It does not want to submit to God's absolute authority or rely on God's absolute mercy. This explains why we should not be surprised that there is a war going on inside between our flesh and God's Spirit. The flesh is responsible for encouraging us to do those things we know we should not do, and prevents us from doing those things that we know we should do. We war within ourselves as we strive to do what is right, always having to battle against what satisfies the flesh rather than the soul. Psalms 27:1 says, "The Lord is my light and my salvation, who shall I fear? the Lord is the strength of my life; of whom shall I be afraid? We would never experience fear generated from within if we would remember this. God is the strength of our lives, our light and our salvation.

Process #3
Exfoliate
(Renewing the Mind)

What is the scriptural reference Romans 12:1 saying to you?

Where does God's transforming power begin it's work first?

What are some of the negative emotions that Satan is responsible for sending? How can *you* prevent his attacks?

What is the identifying mark of the flesh?

Process #4
Astringents
(Forgiveness and Growth)

"But he was wounded for our transgressions, he was bruised for our iniquities: the chastisement of our peace was upon him; and by his stripes we are healed." Isaiah 53:5

Cleansing (exfoliating) is good for the face. It helps to remove dirt on the surface of the skin, but to do deep cleaning, you need to use an astringent that aids in removing any left over impurities that the cleansing process has left behind.

Now that you have cleansed and removed the make-up and revealed the real you, there is still some residual matter left. God's Word has revealed who you are and what you are not, now you need to do something to be sure the impurities are completely removed.

The only way to remove this imbedded dirt is to accept Jesus' death on the cross for our sins. Those dead in sin cannot raise themselves to "life". Deeds of sin can only be forgiven by God. Corruption needs a complete cleansing. The physical agony that Jesus endured was the punishment we deserved. He became the sacrificial lamb and died in our stead. By suffering the humiliation of death on the cross, Jesus paid the atoning price for the imbedded dirt that dwelled deep in our souls. Astringent stings as it does it's work to unclog our pores. As the astringent works, we experience "growing pain". Trials and tribulations will continue to come our way, but we must glory in these. Not because we enjoy the pain, but because we know God is using life's difficulties and Satan's attacks to build our character. Jesus died so that our "pores" would be clean of sin. Through His death we were shown the way to new life, then a trade took place, *our sins for His goodness and forgiveness.*

The astringent deep cleans to help us become more Christ like; however, the process is continuous and will not be complete until we see Christ face to face. But knowing that our ultimate goal is to be Christ like, we should be motivated to purify ourselves. To purify means to keep morally straight, free from the corruption of sin (unclogged). God does purify us, but there are actions we must take to remain morally fit. (1 Timothy 5:22; James 4:8 and 1 Peter 1:22) We must put our confidence (trust) in Jesus to forgive our sins, to make us right with God and to empower us to live the way he has taught us.

God does everything to help us be people of beauty and righteousness in a sinful world, but we must endeavor to follow Him.

Process #4
Astringents
(Forgiveness and Growth)

How can the trials we suffer aid us in our spiritual growth?

I Timothy 5:22; James 4:8 & I Peter 1:22 tells us what we have to do in order to receive God's purification. Express your thoughts about these scriptural references.

Diane W. Pheal

Process #5
Toner
(Faith)

"And a woman having an issue of blood twelve years, which had spent all her living upon physicians, neither could be healed of any. Came behind him; and touched the border of his garment: and immediately her issue of blood stanched. And Jesus said; Who touched me? Luke 8:41-45a

Using a toner on the face helps to sooth, heal and refine the skin. Our souls need to be soothed, healed and refined, but the only way we can do this is through our faith in the atoning blood of Jesus Christ. Our faith serves as the toner we need in our lives. Through her faith the woman in the passage was healed. God's forgiveness of our sins is the greatest gift we will ever receive. We need to touch the hem of His garment so we too can be made whole!

When we fail to live up to the expectations of God, when we forget and turn our backs on God, He will let us become unattended, like flaws that develop in our skin when we fail to follow the regimen of taking care of our skin. When God leaves us unattended, we will become infested with all kinds of problems. If we do no let God, in the presence of the Holy Spirit protect and cultivate our lives, we will become desolate people. We must practice using our toner (faith) in our daily lives. "And the Lord said, "If ye had faith as a grain of mustard seed, ye shall say unto this mountain, Remove hence to younder place; and it shall

remove; and nothing shall be impossible unto you."
(Matthew 17:20) A small amount of genuine faith in God
will take root and grow. As it grows, it will begin to spread.
Although the change in our lives will be gradual, faith will
soon produce major results that will uproot and destroy
conflicting loyalties. We don't need more faith, a tiny seed
of faith is enough if it is alive and growing.

It isn't enough to say we believe Jesus will or can take
care of our problems. We need to **act** as if he can. When
we pray about a problem or concern, we need to live as
though it is done. Perseverance in faith brings with it a
reward. If not in this life, most certainly in our hope of
eternal life with Jesus.

It is easy to become discouraged when there are
unpleasant circumstances in our lives or when we take
unimportant situations too seriously. We are quick to say
that person or that situation "stole my joy." But if we look
at life in the right perspective and are living in partnership
with Jesus, our joy *cannot* be stolen. "Be careful for
nothing; but in every thing by prayer and supplication with
thanksgiving let your requests be made known unto God."
(Philippians 4:6) Ultimate joy comes from Christ dwelling
within us. Jesus sent the comforter to sooth all of our fears
and calm all of our doubts. As we are use the toner of faith,
we will also see the effects the "refining" process does. The
refining process frees us from moral imperfections just as
toner for the skin aids in healing it to a state of becoming
pure and almost perfect. During the refining process we
begin to heal from within. All those things that were
damaging us on the inside, hatred, jealousy, misguided
thoughts, evil deeds, selfishness, lack of love for our fellow
man, greed, words that offend and many more are gradually

being removed. As we tone up the inside, the beauty that is replacing the ugly begins to seep out and show itself.

The toner will help sooth, heal and refine us inwardly because God promised to make all rough places smooth and to straighten the crooked paths in our lives. We should never let our faith become hindered by trials and sufferings.

Our faith should be like a tree rooted in the ground. Nothing should be allowed to weaken or attempt to uproot our faith in God. Our faith helps us to see things as though they are. Hebrews 11:1 assures us that "faith is the substance of things hoped for and the evidence of things not seen." During our early years as children of God, we learned that we walk by faith and not by sight. We do not always see the blessings that God has for us right away, but our soul assures us that they are coming if not already manifested. Your faith will keep you moving towards your goal to be more Christ like.

Process #5
(Faith)

What happens when we become unattended by God?

What does it mean to preserve in our faith?

What does Philippians 4:6 tell you about trusting God? How can you make that change today in your life?

When we are healing from within, what things are removed?

What is faith (Hebrews 11:1)? How is your faith?

Process # 6
Moisturizer
(The Holy Spirit)

"Keep me as the apple of your eye, hide me under the shadow of thy wings. Psalms 17:8

Moisturizers are used after a facial or cleansing to nourish and protect the skin. Just as we apply the moisturizer trusting that it will do what the manufacturer states it will do, we need to put that same faith in knowing that God will nourish us through his word and protect us from the enemy's attacks. We need to stay constant in prayer. Just because we experience troubles in our lives does not mean that we are not under God's protection. God's protection has a far greater purpose than protecting us from pain. His protection makes us better servants for him. God often protects us by guiding us through our circumstances, not by helping us escape them.

"Jesus saith unto them, "My meat is to do the will of him that sent me, and to finish his work." (John 4:34). The *"meat"* that Jesus is speaking of is his spiritual nourishment which includes more than Bible study, prayer, and attending church. Spiritual nourishment also comes from doing God's will and helping to bring his work of salvation to completion. Our nourishment does not come only by what we take in, but also by what we put out for God.

In order to do God's will, we must be moisturized with the Spirit. **God sent the Holy Spirit to work in, through and for us.** He does his perfect work as we go through the purification process which aids in making us beautiful on the inside. Everything that was held captive to sin on the inside will be released during the cleansing process.

Offering up sacrifices and going through religious rituals is not enough. God wants his people to have **changed** lives. He wants us to be fair, just, merciful and humble. God wants us to become "living" sacrifices for him. "I beseech you therefore, by the mercies of God, that ye present your bodies a living sacrifice, holy, acceptable unto God, *which is* your reasonable service. (Romans 12: 1)

As we yield unto God our bodies and souls, we will become living sacrifices, not only ready, but excited to be in service for the Lord. We may feel that we are disqualified from serving God because of past mistakes, but serving God is not an earned position. None of us qualified for God's service, but He still asks us to carry out His work. Therefore, we have been given another chance. It is not our hearing of God's Word that pleases Him, but, our responding obediently to *it* that pleases him. God answers the prayers of those who call upon Him. He will always work His will and desires that everyone come to Him, trust Him and be saved.

Process #6
Moisturizer
(The Holy Spirit)

How does God's protection work for his servants in times of crises?

What is the Holy Spirit's responsibility to us, God's children?

What does God want from you?

God does not want us to only hear his word, what are we to do?

Diane W. Pheal

Process #7
Night Cream
(Prayer, God's Word & The Holy Spirit)

"And be not conformed to this world, but be ye transformed by the renewing of your mind, that ye may prove what is that good, and acceptable, and perfect, will of God." (Romans 12:2)

Finally, you apply your night cream which is designed to leave you feeling refreshed and renewed. When you perform this process on a daily basis, your skin becomes transformed from it's previous state to a renewed state.

God wants you to be transformed inwardly! But first, you need to understand the two-sided reality of the Christian life:

- ❖ On one hand we are complete in Christ (our acceptance with him is secure.
- ❖ On the other hand, we are growing in Christ (we are becoming more and more like him)
  - o At the same time, we have the status of Queens and the duties of slaves;
  - o We feel both the presence of Christ and the pressure of sin;
  - o We enjoy the peace that comes from being made right with God, but we still have to face and deal with daily problems as we grow.

If we remember the two sides of the Christian life, we will not become discouraged when we face temptations and problems. Instead, we learn to depend on the power available to us from Christ, who lives in us as the Holy Spirit.

As Christians we are called to "be not conformed to this world" with its behavior and customs. Our behavioral changes begin with the renewing of the mind. It is possible to avoid the behavior of the world and still be proud, selfish, stubborn and arrogant. Only when the Holy Spirit renews, re-educates and re-directs our minds are we truly transformed.

Our mind transformation can be enhanced if we use the word at night, letting it work while we sleep. One of the joys of being transformed is the peace that God's Word gives. "Peace I leave with you, my peace I give unto you, not as the world giveth, give I unto you. Let not your heart be troubled, neither be afraid." (John 14:27) The result of the Holy Spirit's work in our lives is a deep and lasting peace. So where do we stand as those who have been redeemed by the blood of Christ? We have been buried with Him by baptism unto death and raised up from the dead and now walk in "victory and "newness of life."

We can rest at night when we take God's Word to bed with us and wake up feeling refreshed!

Process #7
Night Cream
(Prayer, God's Word & The Holy Spirit)

Review the two sides of the Christian life. What does this say to you?

What are the three R's that are the results of transformation?

What is John 14:27 saying to you?

Diane W. Pheal

The Holy Spirit

"What time I am not afraid, I will trust in thee. In God I will praise his word, in God I have put my trust; I will not fear what flesh can do unto me." Psalm 56: 2—3

"There is therefore now no condemnation to them which are in Christ Jesus, who walk not after the flesh, but after the Spirit." Romans 8:1

The Spirit of Life is in Christ Jesus. This Spirit is the Holy Spirit. He was present at the creation of the world and he is the power behind the rebirth of every Christian. He gives us the power we need to live the Christian life. Romans 5:1 says, "Therefore being justified by faith, we have peace with God through our Lord Jesus Christ." We are going through a daily sanctification process with the Holy Spirit. We walk in the Spirit and not the flesh. Daily we choose or work hard at centering our lives on God. We have made our choice because we know that our continuation in the Lord brings life and peace.

In Romans 7:14-15 Paul enlightens us about the struggle that takes place within our souls. Christians *do* experience a struggle within their souls. We are at war within ourselves because the desires of the flesh are constantly before us. But the saving grace about this is that, the point is not **"war"** but **"victory"**. When you walk by the Spirit, you will not let those bad desires come to maturity, but rather nip them in the bud. Our promise is "victory" over the desires of the flesh and the winner ***will*** be the "*Spirit.*"

We all have evil desires and we can't ignore them. In order for us to follow the Holy Spirit's guidance, we *must* deal with them by crucifying them. When we ignore our sins or refuse to deal with them we reveal that we have not received the gift of the Spirit that leads to a transformed life. When we make the decision to accept Christ, we need to turn from our sins and willingly nail our sinful nature to the cross. This doesn't mean that we will never see traces of our sinful or evil desires again. As Christians, we still have the capacity to sin, but, we have been set free from sin's power <u>over</u> us and no longer give in to it.

We must daily commit our sinful tendencies to God's control, daily crucify them and moment by moment draw on the Spirit's power to overcome them. When we do this, the old "I" is crucified and a new "I" in the flesh lives by faith. You can then say the life **"I"** live in *this* flesh **"I"** live by faith.

God is interested in every part of our lives, not just the Spiritual part. As we live by the Holy Spirit's power, we need to submit every aspect of our lives to God—emotional, physical, social, relationship, etc. "If we live in the Spirit, let us also walk in the Spirit." Paul is saying, if we are saved, we should live like it!

All creation (creatures) are in pain, living in torment and agony. Life on this earth is work that is especially of a painful or laborious nature. Those of us who have the Spirit groan in pain as well. We groan within ourselves as we wait patiently on deliverance from God.

As we painfully work to transform our inner selves, we need to realize that the Holy Spirit helps us in our weaknesses, even in our prayer life. There are times when we just don't know how to pray for what we need. It is at this time that the Holy Spirit makes intercession on our behalf. Our Father and the Spirit knows just what we need before we ask or even before we can truly understand what it is we need. *We know something needs to happen, but we just don't know what.* Therefore we are encouraged to pray, because in Ephesians 3:20, 21, "we are reminded that God is able to do exceeding abundantly above all that we ask for or even think."

When we live each day controlled and guided by the Holy Spirit, the words of Christ will be in our minds and hearts, and the love of Christ will be behind our actions and the power of Christ will help us control selfish desires.

God's love towards us is total. It reaches every corner of our lives. It is _long_ because it continues the length of our lives. It is _deep_ because it reaches the depths of discouragement, despair and even death. It is _wide_ because it covers the breadth of our own experiences and then reaches out to touch those we come in contact with. It is _high_ because it rises up to meet our celebration and elation in Him. God's love is eternal and his wisdom and power are supreme. *We are never lost in God's love!*

Diane W. Pheal

Faith

"Now faith is the substance of things hoped for, the evidence of things not seen." Hebrews 11:1

Our faith can be described by two words: confidence and certainty. These two qualities need a secure beginning and ending point. The beginning point of faith is believing in God's character—he *is* who he says. The end point is believing in God's promises—he *will* do what he says. True faith is demonstrated when we believe God will do what he says even though those promises have not yet materialized.

Our words are measured by the quality of our character. If your friends trust what you say, it is because they trust you. If you trust what God says, it is because you trust him to be the God he claims to be. If you doubt God, you doubt the integrity of God himself. If you believe God is truly who he says he is, then believe what he says. James 1:17a says, "Every good and perfect gift comes from above." So when we wonder if there is anyone we can trust, remember that God is consistent and completely trustworthy. Those of us who believe in Jesus but encounter situations that cannot be understood must continue to trust that God will work in the best way for their deliverance.

Many of us who have true faith are weak in it because we do not exercise it. The analogy to this is like having exercise equipment that is never being used or only used once in a while. The wonderful results cannot be obtained if it just sits there. This applies to our faith as well. Faith has to be exercised on a daily basis. As Christians, we must walk by faith and not by sight. A lack of faith can bring problems, but on the other hand, having faith gives us endurance, opens the door to new resources, grows with exercise, comes alive when we apply scripture to it, is believing the impossible and is shown in our lives as evidence of God's presence. We are saved by God's free gift (grace) through faith. Satisfying God does not come from the works we do, but from whom we believe. Our Spiritual development is built on our affirmation that Jesus is who he claims to be.

As we go through our beautification process, we are admonished to live the Christian life as a "walk of faith." Facts of life and the appearance of feelings often interrupt our faith. But nevertheless, your perseverance of faith brings a reward. We must possess "Active Faith." This faith gives thanks for a promise even though it is not yet performed, knowing that God will do what he says he will do.

Jesus said "I am the resurrection and the life. He who believes in me will live, even though he dies; and whoever lives and believes in me will never die." (John 11:25) To die to self is to live. In order for us to live, we must learn, and, in order to learn, we must hear what God is saying to us. We must be well armed with the word in order to handle worldly cares. Worldly cares are hindrances to our profiting from the Word of God. Human ears hear many sounds, but there is a deeper kind of listening that results in "spiritual understanding." If you honestly seek God's will, you will have "spiritual hearing."

As Christians, we have been crucified with Christ. God looks at us as if we have died with Christ and yet we live, but not of ourselves, but the Christ that dwells in us. This life we live in the flesh, we live by faith in Jesus Christ, the Son of God.

We no longer live to please ourselves, but are or should be spending our lives to please God. *We are brand new people on the inside, we have new life, we are not reformed, rehabilitated or re-educated.* We are **new** creatures living in vital union with Christ.

All you need is faith the size of a mustard seed, nourish it, exercise it and watch it grow. Your faith will help you climb the highest mountain, see you through all the storms of life and solidify your relationship with God.

Diane W. Pheal

Prayer, Praise and Deliverance

"Give ear O LORD to my prayer; and attend to the voice of my supplications. In the day of my trouble, I will call upon you. For you will answer". Psalms 86:6-7

"He shall call upon me and I will answer him; I will be with him in trouble and show him my salvation". Psalms 91:15-16

The most common problems in prayer is not the asking, but asking for the wrong things, or asking for the wrong reason. Our prayers will become powerful when we allow God to change our desires so that they correspond with God's will for our lives. In Jeremiah 11:1-3, God promises peace and prosperity. "Call upon me, and I will answer thee, and show thee great and mighty things, which thou knowest not" (verse 3). God assures Jeremiah that he only has to ask. God is ready to answer our prayers but we must ask for his assistance. Yes, he could take care of our needs without us asking because he knows everything about us, but when we ask, we are acknowledging that he alone is God and we cannot accomplish what we need in our own strength. When we ask, we must humble ourselves, lay aside our willfulness and worry and be determined to obey him.

God says "call me". When we are held captive to our circumstances, this is when our attention usually turns to God. Healing lies not in our deliverance from a problem but in developing a relationship with God in the midst of the problem.

God says "I will answer". God's answer is his answer, yes, no, or wait. When God's answer is not favorable, we can ask him to reveal to us what is hindering us from being in a position to receive the "yes" answer we want. When in an "unfavorable" answer position, it is wise that we wait. We can ask him to evaluate our heart desires and show us which ones are not in keeping with his perfect will for our lives. "No and wait" answers can be very productive for our spiritual growth, even though they are seldom the answers we want. <u>The bottom line is that we can't hurry God and we can't change his mind!</u> God is more interested in our eternal growth, our faith, our obedience, and our character rather than making us happy for the current moment.

Prayer is an offense against Satan's attacks and strongholds.

When we begin to pray with power, the enemy of our souls will come to us questioning "who do you think you are to pray for this or that?" "God will not answer that prayer". Our prayers can be powerful when we pray believing it is done and if our prayer is in the will of God. Our prayers can be rendered anytime, anywhere, and for anyone. James 4:2 says "we have not because we ask not". We must pray with authority against those things that threaten our peace and relationship with God.

"Now this is the confidence we have in Him, that if we ask anything according to His will, He hears us. And if we know that He hears us, we know that we have the petitions that we have asked of Him". 1 John5:14-15

"Praise ye the LORD, Praise, O ye servants of the Lord, praise the name of the LORD. Blessed be the

name of the LORD from this time forth and evermore. From the rising of the sun unto the going down of the same the LORD's name is to be praised, Psalms 113:1—3

To "praise" means to celebrate, to make something bright, to radiate the glory of God. To "glorify" God is to tell of His greatness, of His character as revealed by Him in His scriptures in the Old and New Testaments.

The name of the Lord should always bring praise. Ephesians 5:19—20, "Speaking to yourselves in psalms and hymns and spiritual songs, singing and making melody in your heart to the Lord. Giving thanks always for all things unto God and the Father in the name of our Lord Jesus Christ."

We can thank God for everything that comes our way. This does not mean thanking him for the <u>sin</u> that accompanies <u>evil</u>, but offering thanks for *what* He will bring out of and through it. We must pray that God will make our lives one of <u>*continual*</u> thanksgiving and praise so He will then make "EVERYTHING" a blessing. Then we can sing:

> Praise God from whom all blessings flow,
> Praise Him all creatures below.

You have the most reasons to praise him as you have received His favor and it should be easy and pleasant to speak of our Master. God wants our love, our loyalty and our lives. He desires to have communion with us. We need to be sure we have this relationship with Him and do all we can to live up to the requirements. Through obedience, we acknowledge His claim upon our lives. Disobedience is a blatant rejection of that claim which carries with it punishment.

God has supreme, unlimited power over the entire universe. He creates, He preserves, He governs. God is sufficient to handle our lives. Every breath depends on the Spirit He has breathed into us. We should desire to learn more of his plan for us each day. How? Through prayer and supplication. We must give all our needs and desires over to Him, knowing that He is able to sustain us, strengthen us and supply our needs daily. The formula is: **P + P = D (PRAYER + PRAISE = DELIVERANCE).**

- ❖ Let us always praise the Lord for He is the Creator of all things
- ❖ Let us not be ashamed to give Him credit and be committed to praising Him as long as we live

Finally, when we take time to praise God, we find a refreshing moment that makes all the difference in our daily lives. In that moment you can say the following prayer:

"This is the day that the Lord hath made, I will rejoice and be glad in it." Psalms 118:24

…encourage yourself:

I believe I can successfully handle all problems that will arise today. I feel good physically, mentally and emotionally. It is wonderful to be alive. I am grateful for all that I have had, for all that I now have and for all that I shall have. Things aren't going to fall apart. God is here and He is with me and He will see me through. I thank God for every good thing!

…pledge:

Every day of my life I will conceive myself as living in partnership and companionship with Jesus Christ. He is with me—right by my side. I place this day, my life, my loved ones, my work in the Lord's hands. Whatever happens, whatever results, if I am in the good Lord's hands, it is the Lord's will and it is good!

Personal note: This is my personal daily prayer, encouragement and pledge. I keep it in my bathroom, right by my mirror. Every morning I have an opportunity to look at this as I am preparing for my day. I have done this for more than 15 years. It helps me to strengthen up for the day and humbles my soul. It reminds me of who is in charge of my life and my difficulties. It has always been a source of comfort and encouragement to me and I want to share it with you.

Remember: Prayer + Praise = Deliverance

Diane W. Pheal

Don't Run From God
Jonah—Chapters 1—2

Doing God's will sometimes means waiting patiently. While we wait, we can love God, serve others and tell them about him. Waiting for God is not easy. Often, blessings cannot be received unless we go through the trial of waiting.

You remember the story of Jonah, a prophet who hated the powerful and wicked Assyrians. Jonah was called by God to warn the Assyrians that they would receive judgment if they did not repent. Jonah *didn't* want to go to Nineveh so he *tried* to run from God. But God has ways of teaching us to obey and follow him. In his flight, (he apparently didn't have a guilty conscience about not doing God's will) Jonah was swallowed by a large fish and remained there until he agreed to do the will of God. Note here that the absence of guilt does not mean we are doing the right thing. Because we can deny reality, we cannot measure obedience by our feelings. Instead, we must compare what we do with the standards God gives us to live by.

Jonah in the belly of a great fish is described as a miraculous event. The scripture says that God "prepared" a great fish to swallow up Jonah meaning that the fish was a part of God's teaching process for Jonah. The creature was "conditioned to do Jonah no harm, meaning that the digestive system had be locked by the power of God. Jonah was able to think about what he had done and prayed a prayer of thanksgiving asking God to deliver him.

We too are in our "great bellies" of affliction and should pray a prayer to thanksgiving and deliverance.

We can pray anywhere and at any time and be certain that God will hear us. Our sin is never to great and our situation is never to difficult for God.

You cannot seek God's love and run from him at the same time. Jonah soon realized that no matter where he went, he couldn't get away from God. Before he could return to God, he had to stop running away from him.

If we want more of God's power, we must be willing to carry the responsibilities he gives us. God is able to use even our mistakes to help others come to know him. It may be painful, but admitting our sins can be a powerful example to those who don't know God.

When you know God wants you to do something, don't run, God may not stop you! God answers the prayers of those who call upon him. He will always work his will and desires that everyone come to him, trust him and be saved. If we obey God's Word, he will gently lead us. God's harsh judgment of destruction is reserved for those who persist to be rebellious. When we respond in obedience, God will be gracious to show us mercy.

Epilogue

Ephesians 4—Oneness with Christ

One process of the facial works better if used in conjunction with the others. If you want beautiful skin, you have to do all of the processes. If you want a "beautiful soul" you have to be a part of the body of Christ.

As you renew yourself, others will see it and want what you have. When you share the "Soul Beautiful" process, it teaches others and they then share with others. Each time the someone goes through the process, they draw closer to the Father. We are all a part of the body of Christ with uniqueness and particular "body functions." The beauty that we each possess includes special gifts, talents and/or abilities.

God loves us all and sees the beauty in us all. God has chosen us to be Christ's representatives on earth. In Ephesians 4:2 Paul challenges us to *live worthy* of the name "*Christian*" meaning "Christ's one." We must live humble, gentle, patient, understanding and peaceful lives. This is why it is so important to keep our inner selves **beautiful and cleansed**.

We must live in unity with our sisters and brothers. No one is ever going to be perfect here on earth, so we must accept and love other Christians in spite of their faults.

Ephesians 4:7 tells us that all believers in Christ belong to one body. Verse 5 says, "One Lord, one faith, one baptism." Verse 6 says, One God and Father, of all, who *is* above all, and through all, and in you all." When the scripture says, "through all," it shows God's active presence in the world and in the lives of believers. We are all united under one head, who is Christ.

God has given us all that we need to be a part of his body. He sent his son to die for us, so that we can live for him. In order to live for him, we must be willing to give of ourselves completely. In order to do this we must purge ourselves from the "old" self, and, we can do this by daily cleansing. No person who has given their life to Christ becomes a lone solider in God's army. Each of us has been given a charge and it is up to us to accept and live up to that charge as true members of God's body. For we must know that we are at war with the enemy and will continue to be in battle with him until Christ's return. God assures us that he will be with us as we battle the enemy. He speaks to us through his word and his angels comfort and protect us. We are never left alone to defend ourselves because we are "one with Christ." We are all an important part of God's plan for the world. We are his hands, feet and lips.

You have been given the cleansing process to help you become more beautiful inwardly. It is your personal choice now to make the decision to give everything over to God for refinement. Something more precious than gold will come forth.

You've heard God's sweet voice calling out to you, now all you have to do is to respond. Don't delay, be obedient to his voice and receive your blessings.

God is waiting to hear from you!

JOURNAL

Diane W. Pheal

How to Use Your Journal

After you have read this book, it is suggested by the author that you keep it in a visible location, ready to record your daily prayers, thoughts, praises, and blessings. Review your entries on a weekly basis to encourage yourself and see how the Lord's cleansing process is working. Record your stumbles, pray, get up and continue. At the end of the month, see how far the Lord has brought you and then get in the habit of keeping a spiritual growth journal.

Scripture is taken from the New International Version and the King James version of the Holy Bible.)

Day One

"Submit yourselves, then, to God. Resist the devil, and he will flee from you." James 4:7

_____
_____
_____
_____
_____
_____
_____
_____
_____
_____
_____

Day Two

"In the same way the Spirit helps us in our weakness."
Romans 8:25a

_____
_____
_____
_____
_____
_____
_____
_____
_____
_____

Day Three

"Blessed are all who fear the Lord, who walk in his ways." Psalm 128:1

_____

_____

_____

_____

_____

_____

_____

_____

_____

_____

_____

Day Four

"Let another praise you, and not your own mouth; someone else, and not your own lips." Proverbs 27:2

_____
_____
_____
_____
_____
_____
_____
_____
_____
_____
_____

Day Five

"How beautiful on the mountains are the feet of those who bring good news." Isaiah 52:7a

_____
_____
_____
_____
_____
_____
_____
_____
_____
_____

Day Six

"The wisdom of the prudent is to give thought to their ways." Proverbs 14:8

_____

_____

_____

_____

_____

_____

_____

_____

_____

_____

Day Seven

"But the fruit of the Spirit is love, joy, peace, patience, kindness, goodness, faithfulness, gentleness and self control." Galatians 5:22

_____

_____

_____

_____

_____

_____

_____

_____

_____

_____

Day Eight

"Your eye is the lamp of your body. When your eyes are good, your whole body is also full of light." Luke 11:34

_____

_____

_____

_____

_____

_____

_____

_____

_____

_____

_____

Day Nine

"Wisdom is the principal thing: *therefore* get wisdom: and with all thy getting get understanding." Proverbs 4:7

_____

_____

_____

_____

_____

_____

_____

_____

_____

_____

_____

Day Ten

"Give us this day our daily bread" Matthew 6:11

_____
_____
_____
_____
_____
_____
_____
_____
_____
_____

Day Eleven

"Jesus said, I am the resurrection and the life." John 17:25a

_____

_____

_____

_____

_____

_____

_____

_____

_____

_____

_____

Day Twelve

"For in him we live, and move and have our being."
Acts 17:28a

_____

_____

_____

_____

_____

_____

_____

_____

_____

_____

_____

Day Thirteen

"Therefore being justified by faith, we have peace with God through our Lord Jesus Christ." Romans 5:1

_____

_____

_____

_____

_____

_____

_____

_____

_____

_____

Day Fourteen

"And we know that all things work together for good to them that love God, to them who are the called according to *his* purpose." Romans 8:28

_____
_____
_____
_____
_____
_____
_____
_____
_____
_____
_____

Day Fifteen

"My grace is sufficient for thee: for my strength is made perfect in weakness." 2 Corinthians 12:9

_____
_____
_____
_____
_____
_____
_____
_____
_____
_____
_____

Day Sixteen

"Be strong in the Lord, and in the power of his might."
Ephesians 6:10

_____
_____
_____
_____
_____
_____
_____
_____
_____
_____
_____

Day Seventeen

"Wherefore take unto you the whole armour of God."
Ephesians 6:13

_____
_____
_____
_____
_____
_____
_____
_____
_____
_____
_____

Day Eighteen

"Study to show thyself approved unto God, a workman that needeth not to be ashamed, rightly dividing the word of truth. 2 Timothy 2:15

_____
_____
_____
_____
_____
_____
_____
_____
_____
_____
_____

Day Nineteen

"Whether you turn to the right or to the left, your ears will hear a voice behind you, saying, "This is the way; walk in it." Isaiah 30:31

_____

_____

_____

_____

_____

_____

_____

_____

_____

_____

Day Twenty

"We must go through many hardships to enter the kingdom of God. Acts 14:22

_____

_____

_____

_____

_____

_____

_____

_____

_____

_____

Day Twenty-One

"Blessed are all who wait for him! Isaiah 30:18

_____
_____
_____
_____
_____
_____
_____
_____
_____
_____

Diane W. Pheal

Day Twenty-Two

"Now we know that if the earthly tent we live in is destroyed, we have a building from God, an eternal house in heaven, not built by human hands. 2 Corinthians 5:1

_____
_____
_____
_____
_____
_____
_____
_____
_____
_____
_____

Day Twenty-Three

"Imitate those who through faith and patience inherit what has been promised." Hebrews 6:12

_____

_____

_____

_____

_____

_____

_____

_____

_____

_____

_____

Day Twenty-Four

"Stand fast therefore in the liberty wherewith Christ hath made us free." Galatians 5a

_____

_____

_____

_____

_____

_____

_____

_____

_____

_____

Day Twenty-Five

"Reckon it nothing but joy…whenever you find yourself hedged in by the various trials, be assured that the testing of your faith leads to power of endurance." James 1:2-3

_____
_____
_____
_____
_____
_____
_____
_____
_____
_____
_____

Diane W. Pheal

Day Twenty-Six

"Surely I am with you always." Matthew 28:20

_____
_____
_____
_____
_____
_____
_____
_____
_____
_____
_____

Day Twenty-Seven

"If you can"?...Everything is possible for him who
believes." Mark 9:23

_____

_____

_____

_____

_____

_____

_____

_____

_____

_____

_____

Day Twenty-Eight

"Let my soul live, and it shall praise thee." Psalms
119:175

_____
_____
_____
_____
_____
_____
_____
_____
_____
_____
_____

Day Twenty-Nine

"That is why, for Christ's sake, I delight in weaknesses, in insults, in hardships, in persecutions, in difficulties. For when I am weak, then I am strong." 2 Corinthians 12:10

_____
_____
_____
_____
_____
_____
_____
_____
_____
_____

Day Thirty

"Make a joyful noise unto the Lord." Psalms 100:1

_____
_____
_____
_____
_____
_____
_____
_____
_____
_____

About The Author

Diane Pheal was born and raised in Memphis, TN where she currently resides. She is the mother of two grown boys and three grandchildren. She teaches an Adult women's Sunday School Class at her church, heads the Drama Department and is the founder of the Women Walking Wisely fellowship in her church (a bible study growth group). She currently works as the Assistant to the Chief Medical Office of a local insurance company. This is Diane's first published writing. Although, this is not *her* work, this is the work of the Lord. He used Diane as a vessel to carry His message. Wording is simple, leaving nothing to wonder about. All praises go to God!